Nudging you Gently Towards More
Organised Paperwork...
Living & Dying Neatly

Dying To Declutter

A Twist on Decluttering

Tracy Hammond
&
Rebecca Crayford

If you do nothing else with our book, please just read the first two pages.

This is a decluttering book with a twist.

We asked family and friends what state their household or personal paperwork was in.

'I do what I have to do'
'It's all over the place, but I have better things to do with my time'
'Who cares about that'?
'Pretty ok, I guess'
'Boring!'

Then you die. Perhaps suddenly. Unexpectedly. So, we asked, 'would your loved ones be able to find all the information required to deal with the legal formalities at such a distressing time?'

'Er no', was the common answer.

And, we went on. 'If your significant other/partner died, would you know where to find everything you need to deal with this, at such

a sad and upsetting time? Passwords to access laptops and phones for vital information? Do you know where all the bank accounts are?

We were met with silence.

So, there is no better message than this:

It pays to have paperwork in order, not only to relieve stress so that you can live your life to the full, but to go a little way to ease the stress on those you leave behind in death. Let's all strive to live and die neatly.

Contents

PREAMBLE

Dotting the Is

Crossing the Ts

Popping the Ps

"Popping your clogs" is inevitable. There we have said it. What an opener to a book.

Sorry about that. Actually, we're not sorry.

The journey to creating this book for you has been full of every emotion imaginable.

We're both in our 50s and have completed a fair chunk of our lives and are now reaching for the orange segments. This feels like a great analogy for those of a similar age who remember school netball matches. Short PE skirts, those big pants and the orange segments at half time? Anyway, it has dawned on us that, as we are now well into the second half of our lives, we want a more organised life with more leisure time.

We want to slow down more, stop rushing. Possessions aren't so important to us anymore. We want to spend more quality time with our parents. Not only are we still parenting our children but we may begin to 'parent' our parents. And we mean that in a tender way. Not a negative way.

Joy is found in the family, in nature (the stuff we thought boring when we were younger), and a simpler way of living is more appealing.

This is where we are now, but the situation applies to anyone at any age. Had we known what we now know, we would have been more organised earlier on in our day to day lives so that being organised became a way of life rather than a last-minute scramble.

By being more organised, and following our process, our gift to you is more time, less stress, and less muddle. That tickles our hearts. And there is that additional bonus for you - the small gift to your loved ones of organised paperwork, when you pass away.

We started this work late in 2019 and little did we realise something with a "P" would barge into our lives the following year. Yes, the Pandemic. Hasn't it changed everything that we thought of as normal? Hasn't it shaken us all to the core? And made us think. No longer can we take things for granted. It has been a sad time for many of us.

As an aside, hold the thought of that letter P.

Through this time, Tracy's partner lost his father so she went through the distress with him as well as the stress he was under, sorting out his father's estate. Where are the passwords? I can't get into his iPad? Where's the V5 log book for the car? To name but a few of the issues that cropped up due to the current digital world we find ourselves living in. And notice those two words **distress** and **stress.** We can alleviate some of this for you.

Tracy was also, during this time, helping out in a charity shop and saw people coming in with personal effects from loved ones who had passed away. They had no idea what to do with these things, their worth, their sentimental value. They just knew they had to clear things out. It was really sad to see potential memories bagged up, the donor oblivious to the contents and potential sentimental value within that item.

It then provoked a discussion between ourselves. Would we know what to do if our husband/partner died? And the answer was NO.

This light-bulb moment alarmed us when we realised that while we're both very organised, not everyone else is. The impact would be huge if Rebecca's husband or Tracy's partner died suddenly, without us knowing where all their passwords and paperwork were stored. We would be stumped. So, the idea for this book was born.

We had uncovered a serious stress inducing problem that we didn't know existed. We originally just wanted people to be more organised to relieve stress and save time in life.

But then it dawned on us that if we don't get organised, we would be leaving a dreadful situation for our loved ones if we died suddenly. Shouldn't we all be organised in life so that we are organised when we die? Don't we owe that to our loved ones who have to pick up the pieces at what is already a stressful time?

Knowing that those left behind would know where to find all the paperwork and 'stuff', enabling them to deal with matters with far less stress and anxiety than if everything was in a mess, can only be a good thing. We shouldn't forget the fact that helping our parents organise their affairs too can make their lives much easier and then eventually ours. Are you getting the picture? There are many benefits to come from this.

To quote someone we met recently:

'My mum has a death box and when she dies, I will know exactly where to find all her paperwork. In the box! Mum loves it and proudly carries it under her arm when she has to do something in it. I used to find it sad but I don't anymore. That's life, so to speak!'

Are you with us so far?

- The investment of a few hours, now, to get yourself organised will free up so much of your time to 'live'. You will know where everything is. Everything is up to date. Everything is tidy. Deep joy!
- With all your paperwork in one place. Your life will be decluttered. Memories stored, shared and not lost. Your legacy will be enjoyed and a little easier to bear when *the time comes.*

Enjoy the organising and 'doing'. Decluttering, whether it be your paperwork or 'stuff' in the home, is known to destress, reduce chaos and muddle. And it frees up space – both physically and mentally. Trust us, headspace is a joy.

So, what about the P?

Well, it's all about progressing through the Ps. Check out our Chapter headings – some will make you smile! We have tried to inject some humour into this where we can.

This whole process, for some reason, did make us reflect on our childhoods and growing up in the '60s '70s and it conjured up all sorts of memories and laughter – we are going to share a few of those too. Keep a look out for them.

Back to the digital age and the 'now'.

To run alongside the book, we have created a free Facebook community– please come along and join us– the link can be found at the back of the book. You can tap into other people's tips and ideas, share experiences, learn new things and get support in a wide range of things that affect us as we go through life.

SO, BEFORE WE GO ANY FURTHER, WHO ARE WE?

What qualifications do we have in this line of work? Well, officially none, because there are none! But between us we do have over 60 years' experience.

That's right, we have no official qualifications for a 'life more organised'. But we have both spent all of our working lives organising people in their offices and homes. It has become second nature. Add in buckets full of life experience with family, friends and all that life throws at us. And for one of us, several overseas/UK moves with a young family meant learning the importance of keeping all household paperwork up-to-date and in one place so she was always ready to deal with short notice moves and changes at the drop of a hat.

We have suffered the highs and lows of life like everyone else and 100% understand how precious our time is and how fraught life can get at times.

Our goal is to gift each and every one of you with more time and with your days being more organised. No stresses or worries. Safe in the knowledge that everything that needs to be done has been done. Of course, at times we fall off the bandwagon, but life is too short to worry about it so the key thing is to get back up, catch up and move on. Don't look back.

"Be positive, just focus and do it. Take yourself forward to how life will be when you have done this. You will sleep easier knowing that you have done everything you can."

Tracy and Rebecca

REBECCA CRAYFORD

When I first started working nearly 30 years ago, my boss had the most amazing memory. He was organised, never forgot anything, and was on time for every meeting. After a few weeks of working for him, I was intrigued so asked him what his secret was. The answer - he wrote EVERYTHING down so he didn't have to rely on his memory. In this way, he could think clearly about his work without being distracted by the millions of things he had to remember. I became a 'list person' there and then and have never looked back!

Now a mum of two and juggling school, work and home, my lists and notebooks are my lifeline.

I also run a lifestyle management business helping clients manage their time. I love helping other people free up their time - after all isn't that what life is all about?

www.rebeccacrayford.co.uk

TRACY HAMMOND

Organised is my middle name after a lifetime of moving around both in the UK and overseas, as a military wife. I can pack up a house, change addresses, sort out new schools, cars, vets, visas in my sleep. And the secret to all of this is being organised.

As a PA and running businesses for 30 years, a mum of two and always wanting to get out and do things, keeping organised to keep ahead was and still is the way I am able to do this. I have the time to enjoy being with my family and friends. I can leave the house on time because I know where my keys are! Boring I hear you say, not a life lived on the edge.

And rolling back the years, I loved Shirley Conran's 'Superwoman' book which I borrowed constantly from the library. How could this woman be so organised? I loved it! I have obviously suppressed this love of organisation since childhood.

I now work mainly in owner managed businesses. By outsourcing to me, they can scale up their business, spend more time with the family or simply just 'be'.

www.tracyhammond.co.uk

"Our lives flow now and we would not change a thing. There are hiccups along the way but the key is to keep getting back on track.

So, let's whip open the kimono, pull up our big girl pants and get organised!"

REBECCA AND TRACY

Chapter 1

The Purpose

&

The Process

When we were growing up, if you wanted to 'phone a friend' and have a good old chinwag without mum and dad listening, it involved a 5p coin and a trip to the phone box.   And waiting outside if someone was already in there!

And if you knew someone you didn't want to speak to was going to ring you at home, you took the phone off the hook.

The purpose of this book is to get you organised in life.
The outcome is that you are then organised when you die too.

- "Does anyone know where the mobile phone contract is?"
- "I need some photo ID and a utility bill for proof of address - anyone? Please?"
- "I want to make a claim on my contents insurance – where did I put the documents that I need?"
- "Where's my bloody driving licence?"
- "Kids be quiet, I am looking for something"
- "Keys? Last seen on the work top?"
- Does anyone know dad's password so we can access his computer?

And so it goes on.

On a day-to-day basis, the time and effort we spend by not being organised can be immense. Not to mention frustrating and unnecessary.

When you add up all the minutes here and there, over a day, a week, a month it can end up being hours, and, quite frankly, it's a waste. Time is precious.

Wouldn't you rather be enjoying a cup of coffee with a friend, reading a book or visiting a relative, safe in the knowledge that your house is in order and your paperwork is all up to date? We know we would.

Like a tap left running with all that water pouring down the drain. There goes your time, drip, drip, drip...

Not anyone's time, but YOUR precious time.

We are all gifted the same amount of time each day. And it is down to each and every one of us to decide how we use it – whether that be in a useful and then enjoyable fashion, or in a wasteful way.

Just stop and think for a moment what you could do with more time. Why not think big?

- Join that yoga or Pilates class
- Enrol on a degree course
- Learn a new skill
- Train for a marathon
- Longer dog walks in the great outdoors
- Enjoying a coffee with friends and having time to 'smell the coffee'
- Getting the sewing machine out and become a 'Sewing Bee' or dusting off the paddleboard

Some groundwork now to help you to become more organised will reap **YOU** time for the rewards **YOU** choose for **YOURSELF**.

For some, it may be that a few organisational tweaks are needed here and there.

For others, a major organisational overhaul.

But either way, let's just DO IT. And we can do it together.

We promise, you will feel amazing when all the tasks are ticked off and your checklists completed.

Then, cue to cartwheeling out the front door to do whatever it is YOU want to do with everything administratively in place, and time on your hands.

Are you still with us? Let's look at the benefits:

- Number 1 **MORE TIME TO LIVE**
- Number 2 **LESS STRESS FOR YOU IN LIFE**
- Number 3 **EASING THE DISTRESS FOR THOSE LEFT BEHIND WHEN YOU DIE**

FOCUS ON THE PROCESS!

This is a book giving you an overview of what needs to be done and is not exhaustive. There are bits you don't need to do as well as bits you will think of, that we haven't, after all we are only human. This is about getting you thinking and starting to take action.

So, jump in with us and enjoy the ride because, if you approach this with an 'if I must?' attitude it's going to be a bore and tedious.

We highly recommend you get and keep a positive 'can do' mindset.

The Process

- Make sure you have a place ready to store your paperwork (if you don't already) – it could be in a box, in a filing cabinet, or in a bag – wherever works best for you, but the key thing is that everything should be in one place. (Further tips in Chapter 2 – Pointers).
- If you are fully or partially digital then create some folders and sub folders on your computer to store your documents.
- Think about appointing your 'trusted person' who will know this place and where everything is kept for future reference.
- Work through the book in your own time. There is no mad dash, no rush. You may want to do a chapter at a time and work through it methodically, or dip in and out as and when the mood takes you. Whichever way you choose, it is absolutely fine. You may go 'hell for leather' at it and then need a breather and some water – that is fine too!
- Make sure you read the 'Pointers' chapter before you start.
- Try to LOVE dealing with your paperwork - it will make this process so much better, not to mention satisfying.
- Keep focusing on how you will feel when all of this is in place and you are organised.

- Find time that works for you to deal with paperwork. We are early birds so we use the hour before everyone else is up and at it - it's the best time for us to go about uninterrupted and do the things that need doing. Stick to your time. 10 minutes daily? An allotted evening? Sunday morning? Whatever works for you but in the early days stick to this scheduled time to get to where you want to be, with regards your paperwork, and to form new habits. Write it in your diary and treat it like an appointment.
- Join our Facebook community – the link can be found at the back of the book. You can ask questions, share your tips, seek advice – all for free.

FAQs

Do we need to retain paperwork in this digital age?

Yes and no. This is your choice.

It is good to get as digital as possible (as in saving your documents on your computer), for many reasons, but some of us still use/love paper and will only use paper. Some of us aren't digitally minded at all and some do not have a computer - and don't even want to get one. And that is fine. Being fully digital scares the pants off us too, if we are honest. So, one size definitely does not fit all. We will cater for each and every one of you. Whether you are using paper, going paperless, fully digital or a little bit of everything.

How can I reduce paperwork?

The digital and online age has hit some of us like a proverbial freight train and being completely paperless is something some of us understandably fret about. In time digital will be the norm for all. At present some generations are between the two. So, let's accept that for now and work with what we have.

Please consider the environment. Think about your use of paper, ink cartridges in printers and so forth when you print off your paperwork. Do you really need to print? Be mindful and recycle where you can.

If you must manage your household using paper, then that is what you must do. But again, please be mindful. Work towards less paper when you are able. That can be a goal. At present we want to get you organised.

When it comes to bills, pay them as they come in so you don't get chased all the way to the red bill, or incur interest on late payments. Then shred (see 'How do I dispose of paperwork safely?' for more on shredding) and recycle. Done! We are sure many have been there and experienced the stress it induces when you realise you have forgotten to pay a bill and face having, for example, the electricity/water/gas cut off. In an ideal world, deal with everything online if you can, so there is no paperwork at all. And being online is quicker and they store all the bills if you need to refer back.

But, can I have a combination of both?

A lot of us do a combination of paper and online. Banking online and paying bills being the common ones. However, not as many of us are 'filing' our paperwork digitally. By this we mean scanning documents and then saving them on your computer using a filing system similar to a physical filing system to ensure they can be retrieved with ease. That is food for thought and means a bit more effort with the additional scanning and uploading. But it can be done and will eventually make you 'paperless' (think of all the space it would save too). There are lots of great scanning apps for your phone and computer these days and it can be done pretty painlessly, so don't be put off giving it a go. A Google search will bring up a host of them. With regards to bills, they are filed online for you by the relevant company, so you can always rest in the knowledge that you can refer back anytime you wish. Paperwork received by email, could be neatly filed online by you for retention.

When at the cash point or in the shops don't take receipts unless absolutely necessary.

And junk mail – don't get us started! Straight into the recycling please. Or even better, you can opt out of junk mail by logging onto the Royal Mail website:

https://www.royalmail.com/sites/default/files/D2D-Opt-Out-Application-Form-2015.pdf

How do I dispose of paperwork safely?

Shredding and recycling. Please don't simply recycle anything into your 'green bin' that can potentially identify you, is sensitive or contains information you wouldn't want people to see. This should be shredded.

There are plenty of shredders on the market at various price scales that offer different security levels when it comes to the shredded paper. It can be shredded into strips or fine particles - it is down to you and we won't go into that here. Google is your friend!

Then the shredding can then go into your recycling bin.

So how does this save time?

A big part of what we do, in our 'day jobs' is freeing up time for our clients but also to help them avoid doing too much. After all, why do more than you need to? What's the saying?

'Work smarter not harder'

By being organised you WILL have less to do in the long run. But, in the early days of getting started and getting to that point, there will be more to do, but that will ease as your paperwork becomes more organised, we promise.

So, we are going to focus in the main on our personal and household paperwork and administration. It won't go away. And of course, as we have already alluded to, a lot of this is now done online so we will cover that too. You can ignore it and stay in chaos. Your choice.

There are many amazing people out there who cover decluttering the physical contents of our homes so we will leave that to the likes of Marie Kondo and now Stacey Solomon. It is worthwhile doing this of course, but in this book, we will focus on paperwork and admin because we have no choice but to accept that paperwork is part and parcel of life. None of us gets taught how to deal effectively with paperwork and it does cause unnecessary stress when it piles up and needs action. And it needn't be like that.

So, let's get back on track. We promise if you work through the book and get yourself into new habits, that:

- dealing with paperwork will become a way of life
- everything is in one place
- you will be able to put your hand to anything – and quickly too

- you will be in a permanently organised state
- appointments will not be forgotten
- you will have TIME

We will get you from chaos to freedom in no time at all to live the life you choose.

From renewing your car insurance on time, to booking the gas man. Applying for a passport way before you go on holiday, to needing to update your CV, booking a dentist appointment and then not forgetting to go because you didn't make a note in your diary. And filing it all away so you can find it again.

You can do this!

Chapter 2

Pointers

We are going to talk about notebooks and with that in mind ...

For those of a certain age, do you remember covering your exercise books in brown paper at school? And then not wanting to write in your new books?

LET'S GET STARTED WITH TOOLS OF THE TRADE

We cannot stress enough that this is a very important part of the Process. This will arm you with the necessary 'bits and bobs' you need to work through the Chapters.

** We have also added some BONUS
time saving hacks as well **

You will need some 'tools of the trade' and if needs be, have a budget for these items so you don't overspend or better still, reuse what you already have. Speaking from joint experience, we can spend, spend, spend on stationery and have to continually rein ourselves in. We love a new notebook.

Also, anything we refer to here that you feel we 'breeze over' or that 'scares the pants off you', then please remember our Facebook community. Perhaps the mention of 'back ups' freaks you out? Digital filing? Just ask the question in the Facebook community and you will get an answer or solution from us in there.

Also, as you work through this, why not sort your significant other/partner's stuff out (if you want to and they allow it of course - we are not saying you should do their work at all). And how about your children's stuff too? One swoop in the household to mop it all up in one go. How fabulous would that be?

STORAGE FOR YOUR PAPERWORK

This is the very heart of what we are all about. Somewhere to store your paperwork so it is *all in one place* and you know exactly where to find it. And, when you die, your trusted person will know where to find it. It can be filed in a cabinet, concertina file, shoebox, carrier bag. Wherever! Put it away and make sure this person knows where it is for that time of need.

You will also need to consider access and storage of your online files too, by way of folders and sub folders. More on that later on in the book and again, make sure your trusted person will be able to access these.

Don't let any of this freak you out. We are here with you all the way through this book and then out there online.

SAFE

A quick word! Some people have a safe in the house, some may want a safe. It's a thought for storage but make sure your trusted person knows or, you have written somewhere, how to access the safe. And if you have a safe, check that it is fire proof.

DIARY

Whether that be a paper diary, a calendar on the wall, an online diary - whatever works for you. This is to record appointments, renewal dates as and when they crop up. Oh, and to add in birthdays and anniversaries. Remember to transfer all of that information into your new diary each year. (A good job for a rainy afternoon in late December, with a nice cup of tea and piece of Christmas cake).

IMPORTANT ADVICE – We cannot stress enough how important a diary is. Have a system in place to remind you of:

- Renewal dates for policies and insurance
- "Check in" dates. These are reminder chunks of time you allocate on a regular basis to go through your

paperwork/digital filing to make sure there is nothing that needs your attention. Think of password changes, PIN changes, new purchases of value that need the receipts filed, scanned documents that may need filing are examples.

- Birthdays, anniversaries, medical appointments and so forth.

TIP - Talking of birthdays, why not have an old shoebox with a stash of cards for various occasions so you are never caught out? And if you want to be really organised, some stamps in that box too. In fact, why not chuck in some wrapping paper whilst you are at it? Keep some bottle bags, inexpensive candles, body/hand lotion for when you get caught out and need a quick gift. And it's important that you know where your addresses are kept.

TIP - You can send cards online if you wish. There are many fabulous websites out there to enable you to do this. If you type a search into Google you will find so many. Examples are below to give you an idea but do 'search' around the internet to find something that you like. We are not endorsing these sites, we're just giving you some ideas of what you are searching for.

www.moonpig.com

www.Paperlesspost.com

www.jacquielawson.com

TIP - Keep some old-fashioned notelets. If you keep RIP dates, for example, then it is lovely to send a little note through the good old-fashioned mail at such a poignant time. It will mean a lot and there are plenty of other times a card through the mail will hit a spot.

We need to get back on track, there's a lot to do.

PINS & PASSWORDS

We are going to put this in very early on. Our lives are full of passwords, PINs, access codes and so forth. We cover this later on in the book but at this stage, find a way to store this information. It could be in a book (there are many password books for sale now), or on a spreadsheet. You could also consider an online Password Manager. We would advise that this information is held away from the paperwork file for obvious reasons. Also, make sure the person you trust will be able to find where the passwords are kept. Please note that your trusted person should be legally allowed to access your accounts.

And REMEMBER, each time you change anything, update your information.

STORAGE OF YOUR LONG-TERM PAPERWORK

You will have one location for your day-to-day paperwork and files. Your PINs and passwords may now be stored somewhere else, if you decide to do this, as above.

However, your long-term paperwork, such as your property deeds, old tax returns, archived documents may well be somewhere else again because it will rarely be accessed. So please ensure you have a note of this location in your file too so that everything can be found with ease by your trusted person.

NOTEBOOKS

Let's find a way of taking notes and writing our 'to do' lists.

A notebook and pen in your bag or by your bed, or how about using 'Notes' or voice notes on your phone? Whatever suits. As you go through the day and think of something, jot it down, or record a message (recording a message can be great when you're on the go – there's nothing worse than squinting at your phone as you're walking while trying to type out a message – just remember to write it down when you get home).

Noting things down can go a long way towards decluttering your mind. Not to mention reducing the stress of trying to remember everything. It is a fantastic tip and an excuse for a new notebook, if nothing else!

Other 'note taking' suggestions that may work for you:

- A notebook by the phone - if you still have a landline - for scribbling down messages. Useful at work more than anything these days.
- A notebook by the bed - this has saved our lives countless times – for when you wake up at 3am and remember something, and then can't go back to sleep in case you forget it. As an aside, it is great for recording dreams or flashes of inspiration that usually pop up in the middle of the night.
- A notebook in the kitchen, or a magnetic pad on the fridge - to note food you need to buy, or items you are running out of.
- Or, take your phone everywhere you go and use Notes or the voice recording app.

These are suggestions only - find a way that works for you. It may be one book that goes everywhere with you in your bag. Or, it's all on your phone.

PAPERWORK – FIND IT!

Before we get to filing, you will need to manage the paperwork that is already in your house and take some action in sorting and decluttering that before we move on.

Look in the backs of cupboards and drawers, grab those letters that have piled up on the kitchen worktop (and open those that are unopened). Take the passports out of the mug cupboard, take the children's appointment cards out of your handbag. Get the drift? Seek out the paperwork and stack it all up in a safe place.

Gather it into three piles as follows and you're good to go:

- **ACTION** immediately if you can (any red bills fall into this category)
- **FILE** away or shred (no action required but useful to keep)
- **PENDING** – non-urgent paperwork - this needs action later

Go on - do it now!

You should then have an '**ACTION**' pile and a '**FILE'** and a '**PENDING'** pile? Well done, you can deal with the 'pending' pile when you have set aside some time to do so. Book time into your diary now and stick to it. You have chosen a time that works for you so there will be no need to avoid doing it and put it off. So, think carefully about a time that you will commit to and won't be interrupted. Treat this like an important appointment.

With regards to mail/post coming in each day to the home, open it immediately if time allows. Throw what is not required into the recycle bin immediately (ensuring no sensitive information goes with it) and add the remaining post into your three piles that you have already started – Action / File / Pending. A very simple process, but it means you won't end up with piles of paper scattered over every surface in the house and this process will be ongoing.

Most of us don't have the time to action paperwork daily so find a place where you can put it away safely, until you do have the time to attend to it. Perhaps an in-tray, drawer or a box specifically for this purpose. But attending to the action paperwork **MUST BE DONE** regularly each week, either one evening or over the weekend. It should take no more than 20 – 30 minutes weekly once you get going. We cannot stress this habit enough for lifelong success. The pending can wait but why not do that at the same time as the action pile?

EMAILS

With emails, try to check them daily. Delete what you don't need, file what you would like to retain and use the 'flag' system to mark up any emails you may wish to return to.

Tracy has a client who simply cannot open her mail because it overwhelms her. So, Tracy goes to her house regularly, to open it, sort it, pay and action what needs to be done and then file it away. AKA The Post Fairy. That may be an extreme case (Tracy does do other work when with her client but that is the first task each time) and it's fine if you are allergic to the post and can afford help. But you have to find a way to deal with it and open it regularly. You

may miss bills or important information if you do not open your
mail but the positive side to all of this is less stress.

TO DO LISTS - some 'Pointers'

- List everything that needs to be done, as you think of it.
- Each day create a 'to do' list. And, don't put anything on there just for the sake of it.
- These are tasks that you are going to do and action. After all you have written them down on your 'to do' list.
- For any larger tasks break these down into bite sized chunks and attack these like a project. Add these smaller tasks to your list each day.
- Think of the 'Power of Three'. If you can do at least three things from your list every day then that is great progress.
- Pomodoro Technique® – basically set a timer for 25 minutes then have a 5-minute break and you carry on in this way until the task is done. It is a time management system and the intervals are the 'pomodoros' (or tomatoes in English!). This is good if you have a chunk of 'to do's' that you think you could do in this timeframe.

ONLINE TO DO LISTS

These apps often offer free unlimited basic usage but you can pay to upgrade for more features if you wish.

We use Trello which is a digital platform used to manage projects, and in our case 'to do' lists in our business as well as home life. Also 'Todoist' which is again an online tool for managing work and life.

www.trello.com

www.todoist.com

FILING SYSTEMS

Paper Filing. This system will depend on the amount of paperwork you have and want to retain and will all be in one place. A concertina file with dividers/sections may work well. You may choose to repurpose a cardboard box or use a filing cabinet, but either way please have somewhere to put your paperwork so it's *all in one place*. This is not the temporary 'PENDING' pile, this is when things have been actioned and are now ready to be put away. That is all we ask of you. Labels, clear wallets, and ways to sort and divide your sections, whatever you want to use. We need to add again that we are 'stationery-aholics' and don't want to encourage you to join us! We have to admit to using some of our free time browsing online for the loveliest filing boxes, shiny diaries or notebooks.

Digital Filing. File online by using folders on your computer for your documents, sorting them into sections or subfolders. Don't just 'dump on the desktop' - treat it like paper filing. There is nothing more frustrating than trawling through a computer searching for documents – however good the search function may be. Documents can be scanned and uploaded. Email attachments can be saved in folders. At this point we need to mention that you need to make sure you are backing up your computer and have a virus checker that is working in the background, so that you do not stand to lose anything. The most common brand names for virus checkers are:

- McAfee (https://www.mcafee.com)
- Norton (https://www.norton.com)
- Bitdefender (https://www.bitdefender.com)

We are not endorsing these sites, we're just giving you some idea as to what you are searching for on Google. These are also widely available on sites like Amazon.

Do your research or pop a question on our Facebook Page for recommendations (link at the back of the book).

The paper and digital filing combo. Some things are digital now and some still on paper so be prepared to be organised in both ways if you have to or indeed want to do it this way.

Going paperless. A great goal, as we have said before, would be to eventually be paperless by being fully online and fully digital. But don't worry yet. Once you are fully organised you can aspire to this but if you are able to do this now, then see if you can achieve it as you work through the book. The planet will love you. Your bank balance will love you. Your mind will be less cluttered.

Paperwork that you don't need to access all the time can be put away somewhere safe, (ours are in recycled cardboard boxes). An example would be the deeds to your house. You need to keep them but will rarely refer to them so why clutter up the house or your filing system with them? Put them away safely in the back of a cupboard, or the attic. But don't forget to write down where you've put them. With this in mind, it might be worth creating an index to keep somewhere in your filing system, or on your computer listing out where all of your paperwork is stored (if not in one place) – just in case.

SUGGESTED FILING SECTIONS FOR DIGITAL AND PAPER FILES

Below are some common file headings:

1. PERSONAL/FAMILY
2. PETS
3. MONEY/PENNIES & POUNDS/FINANCES
4. WORK
5. PROPERTY
6. MEDICAL
7. POSSESSIONS
8. VEHICLES
9. PENSIONS & LEGAL

Let's help you a little bit more, before we move on, with some more generalised organisational tips.

SHOPPING

- Why not have a generic shopping list on your phone/in the front of your notebook/diary that you can refer to each time you go shopping so you don't have to write a list every time? A list of those things you need weekly. We do this and then just make a note of additional bits we need. It saves so much time and effort.

- If shopping online, make use of the stored lists and functions to save time on the supermarket websites. We would encourage everyone to shop online for many reasons. Three in particular.

1. It's kinder to the planet by being a more environmentally friendly way of shopping.
2. Saves money because there is no unnecessary browsing.
3. Saves time.

SHOPPING BAGS

- If going out shopping, keep re-useable bags in the car, in your bag, in the drawer by the door, coat pocket, bicycle basket. Anywhere that you will remember them. This saves time, the planet and money – and reduces your stress levels when trying to get out the door or when reaching the checkout and realising you have bought more than you intended and need another bag. And the key to making this work? Putting them all back in their place when you have finished with them so you can find them again next time, without any further thought.

TIP - Bags going back to the car? Hang them on the doorknob on the inside of the front door, put them by/in your bag, or by your shoes. Just think of somewhere to remind you to do it.

FACE MASK

- As an aside, in this current climate, don't forget to have spare face masks in your bag, car, coat pockets. Do be mindful of the fact that reusable masks need regular washing and that 'use once' face masks must be disposed of properly and not discarded. Think of the environment.

KEYS

- Find a pot, a drawer or some hooks for all your keys, and as you come and go, take them, use them and then put them back where they belong as soon as you come back into the house. It's that simple. You will never have to find a key again. (Do make sure they are in a safe place though and not able to be seen or accessed by someone being close to your door or by looking through your window). And why not think of leaving a key with a neighbour for that 'just in case' situation?

Or, how about a 'key safe' outside that can be accessed with a code that only the family know?

- Also remember to 'train' the family to do this as well! You don't want to be looking for their keys!

Whilst chatting with my father about this book, I asked him where he keeps all his keys. He told me which drawer they're all in, and then very proudly added that he has also labelled every single key in the house (including those for the windows) so there is no confusion as to which locks they all belong to. Such a good idea! Generally speaking, we know which keys belong to the frequently used windows and doors, but what about those that we don't use very often? And what if someone else needed to find the back door key? How would they know? (I should add here for security reasons, that labelled keys should be kept out of sight in a drawer!).

Rebecca

FINAL NAGS

Keep your paperwork safe. Only store what you need, and what you do not need, destroy safely.

Destroying paper is best done by shredding. Only recycle paperwork that cannot identify you in any way.

Declutter your paperwork regularly - shred what is no longer required. As new paperwork and documents come in, destroy the old, straight away. For example, a new insurance document arrives so destroy the old documentation, when you are happy with the new paperwork.

'Out with the old and in with the new!'

Get digital and online as much as you possibly can and when you are confident to do so.

REBECCA'S REMINDERS

❖ Decide what you are going to store your paperwork in and where. It should be accessible and a system that is easy for you to use.

❖ If you have any digital filing, create your folders and sub folders on your computer, in your inbox.

❖ Let your trusted person know what you are doing and where this paperwork and digital files will be stored, at a time of need.

❖ PINs/Passwords. Store these on a spreadsheet, in a book or use an online Password Manager. Remember to leave a note as to where these can be found by your trusted person.

❖ Find a safe place for your Action/Pending/File paperwork before it is put away. This will be ongoing as you add and take things away. And, needs to be accessible daily.

❖ Set up a diary system and use it to diarise everything.

❖ Decide on where you will jot down any notes, things to remember, thoughts – this could be in a notebook, or on your phone. Have this to hand all the time.

❖ Decide on a way to make your shopping list with the least effort (and don't forget to find a place for your re-usable bags).

❖ Have **one** place for your keys – and remember to put them back there when you have finished with them.

❖ Try to become more environmentally friendly by cutting down on paper, recycling and trying to do more online.

❖ Have a supply of new/clean face masks in your car, coat pockets and handbag. And some hand sanitiser.

YOUR ACTION POINTS

1:

2:

3:

4:

5:

6:

7:

Round Up!

You need to have:

… something to store your day-to-day paperwork in that is ready to use and accessible?

… a safe place for this?

… a system set up to store your PINs/passwords?

… somewhere to store long-term documents?

… somewhere on your computer for your digital filing?

*… a trusted person. Someone who knows **NOW** where all of this is or, knows you have left instructions as to where it can all be found.*

Now let's get started!

Chapter 3

Personal

'Text messaging in the 80s was the equivalent of walking to your friend's house, knocking on the door and asking them to come and play!'

You know your full name. And spelt correctly for official documents of course.

You know your date of birth.

You know your marital status.

But...

- Do you know where your birth certificate is? And, if applicable, the birth certificates for your dependents and husband/partner/wife/significant other for that matter?
- Do you have adoption certificates?

- Do you know where your marriage certificate or divorce paperwork is?
- Do you know your NI Number and have a record of this somewhere?

The British Government have a service called **'Tell us Once'** which can be accessed online when someone dies. Below is the information required. We will cover all of this in more detail, later on in the book.

- Date of birth (DOB)
- National Insurance (NI) number
- Driving licence number
- Vehicle registration number
- Passport number

We will focus on DOB and NI in this section. We will cover everything else later in the book and would just say that keeping your Driving Licence on you is a good idea both when out driving and as a form of ID.

QUICK WINS

- If you do know where your documents are then file them NOW in your new filing system under a section titled, for example, PERSONAL/FAMILY. Scan them if you wish and file them digitally as well (but keep the original hard copy).

If you don't know where your birth or marriage certificate are, for example, you can go online and apply for a new one. Rebecca has done this for a client and it's quick and easy to do.

https://www.gov.uk/order-copy-birth-death-marriage-certificate

- For that elusive National Insurance (NI) number? If you can't find it on a payslip or P60, for example, please follow the link below.

https://www.gov.uk/national-insurance/your-national-insurance-number

ONE STEP FURTHER

For official documents, we are often asked for details of our parents – their dates of birth and our mother's maiden name being two such things. Do you know these details? Do your 'grown up' children who may need this info know yours?

Now is the time to set that straight and store that information in a place where you/they can easily retrieve it.

We have the year of our respective parents' birth next to their birth dates so we don't forget. And that is in our diaries. Incidentally, that is also a great way to remember their 'BIG 0' birthdays!

Alternatively write down this information on a piece of paper and file in your PERSONAL/FAMILY section.

This is a short, but very important chapter and a very good place to start.

My father's paperwork is shambolic and I cannot even begin to persuade him to get his affairs in order. I have tried. It's a long story but he lives his life and paperwork is irrelevant to him. He spends summers in England, winters in India.

However... you would think he would have learnt to look after 'paperwork' by now.

He purchased a lottery ticket a few years ago and then misplaced it.

He found it after the 180 days limit.

He lost out on a win of £350,000. Seriously.

So, if nothing else, file away your lottery tickets and check them regularly!

Tracy

REBECCA'S REMINDERS

❖ Think about all the key personal documentation you should have – think birth certificates for you and your family, marriage certificates, divorce papers etc – do you have them? If not, get duplicate copies and file them.

❖ Make sure you have a record of your National Insurance (NI) number.

❖ Do you have a note of your parents' full names, their DOB, their place of birth (occasionally asked for)? If not, ask them (or other members of the family) and make a note.

❖ FILE THE PAPERWORK AWAY

YOUR ACTION POINTS

1:

2:

3:

4:

5:

6:

7:

Chapter 4

Picture of Health

Playing, riding our bikes, building our dens from the moment it was light, until darkness fell, kept us healthy.

We seemed to spend more time together with our families and friends and life felt 'less busy'.

Another section in your filing system will be for 'MEDICAL' or 'HEALTH'. So, let's get stuck in.

- Do you know your NHS number? If you don't, follow this link:

    https://www.nhs.uk/using-the-nhs/about-the-nhs/what-is-an-nhs-number/

- Do you have the details for your doctor, dentist, optician and any other health care professionals stored in your phone or address book for ease of retrieval?

- Are your medical documents all filed together in one place? If not, they need to be gathered up and filed away.

- If you have health insurance, are the documents up to date and filed away with a note of the renewal date?

TIP – Regarding health insurance, you will usually get a renewal notification a few weeks before your renewal date. This is the time to check through the policy and advise the insurers of any changes in circumstances so that your cover is not affected.

- Do you have any appointments, follow ups, check-ups that need booking? Now would be a good time to attend to that and note the date and time in your diary.

TIP – Check with your health care providers to see if you can get text reminders when appointments are due.

- Are any prescription renewals diarised? Have you considered using an online ordering system? In this way you get a reminder to order, and the provider then contacts your GP. Once that is done you will then be prompted to pay for your prescription (if applicable) and then the order is posted to your door. You don't have to remember in future and, it's better for the environment.

The following advice is taken from the NHS website.

Apps and websites that let you order a repeat prescription and use a pharmacy or dispenser of your choice:

- NHS App
- NHS website's repeat prescription service - https://www.nhs.uk/nhs-services/prescriptions-and-pharmacies/the-nhs-website-repeat-prescription-ordering-service/
- Airmid - https://www.tpp-uk.com/products/airmid (selected GP surgeries only)
- Co-op Health - https://www.coop.co.uk/health
- Evergreen Life PHR - https://www.evergreen-life.co.uk/
- myGP - https://www.mygp.com/
- Patally - https://patally.co.uk/
- Patient Access - https://www.patientaccess.com/ (selected GP surgeries only)
- SystmOnline - https://www.tpp-uk.com/products/systmonline (selected GP surgeries only)

Some pharmacies have their own apps and websites, including:

- Boots - https://www.boots.com/online/pharmacy/
- Echo - https://www.echo.co.uk/ (by Lloyds Pharmacy)

- Pharmacy2U - https://www.pharmacy2u.co.uk/

- Organ donation - rules changed on 20 May 2020 so you now have to opt OUT of donating your organs. You may wish to view the amended rules here:

  https://www.organdonation.nhs.uk/get-involved/news/organ-donation-law-change-due-to-come-into-effect-in-england-on-20th-may

The NHS website has so much useful information on all things medical.

https://www.nhs.uk

TIP - We know what the GP Surgery is for and if there is an emergency, we all know about 999. But whilst on medical matters, we wanted to highlight the following very useful services. The detail below is taken from the NHS website.

NHS 111

NHS 111 can help if you have an urgent medical problem and you're not sure what to do.

Local Pharmacists

Pharmacists are experts in medicines and can help you with minor health concerns. As qualified healthcare professionals, they can offer clinical **advice** and over-the-counter medicines for a range of minor illnesses, such as coughs, colds, sore throats, tummy trouble and aches and pains.

REBECCA'S REMINDERS

❖ The important thing here, as you go through and file your paperwork, is to make sure everything is up to date. Filing in date order is also a good tip (as it is with all other paperwork for that matter!). In this instance, it means that you have your health history filed in chronological order.

❖ If applicable. Check your medical insurance is in date and has the right cover in place.

❖ It's helpful to have details of any healthcare professionals on your phone and filed away. Apart from making your life easier, it means that should the need arise, your nearest and dearest can find relevant information easily and quickly.

❖ Look into ordering repeat prescriptions online – that's a quick win and saves lots of time.

❖ Whilst doing this consider working through your partner/significant other/children's paperwork and file. BUT, seek permission first if you are going to do this on behalf of someone else who is of age and therefore able to do this themselves.

❖ Why not use this time to make sure all medical and dental appointments are up to date? Diarise any reminders for example, dental check ups, opticians, routine medical check ups.

❖ FILE THE PAPERWORK AWAY

YOUR ACTION POINTS

1:

2:

3:

4:

5:

6:

7:

Chapter 5

Pets

We remember saying 'mum, I'm just walking the dog'.

And mum saying nothing as the poor old dog went out for the

sixteenth time that day because we had a new boyfriend!

Another section in your filing system will be for 'PETS'. This section can clearly be skipped if it is not applicable to you.

The Government states:

You may get an unlimited fine or be sent to prison for up to 6 months if you don't look after an animal properly. You may also be banned from owning animals in future.

Lots of advice can be found on the following link, with regards the ownership of all sorts of pets.

https://www.gov.uk/caring-for-pets

- Firstly, make sure you are compliant.

- Have you got a note in your diary of, for example, when annual injections, worm and flea treatments are due?

- Do you have the pet's immunisation booklets filed safely somewhere? Remember to take it to each appointment.

- Is this booklet up to date? If not, it can be dropped into the vets for them to update retrospectively and collected at a later date - or they can post it back.

- Do you have your pet insured and if so, when is the renewal date and have you filed the policy paperwork? At each renewal date check for any changes in circumstances so that your cover is not affected.

TIP - Don't forget that pet insurance can cover you for more than just the cost of an illness or the loss of your pet – it can cover you for some third-party damage too, e.g., if your dog ran out in front of a car and caused an accident. As always, check the small print with your provider.

- Do you have contact numbers and details of your pet's 'tribe'? Walker, groomer and so forth? It truly is a dog's life isn't it?

- Do you have text reminders in place for your pet's tribe?

- Do you have a note of any microchip numbers? Great information on the Government websites and updated fine amounts if you do not comply with regards microchip numbers.

https://www.gov.uk/get-your-dog-microchipped

- Pedigree certificates, proof of purchase all filed away so you know where they are?
- Do you have a pet guardian? Do you want to appoint one should something happen to you?

REBECCA'S REMINDERS

❖ File any documentation relating to your pets in one place in a section entitled, funnily enough, PETS!

❖ Diary note any special dates - annual injections, insurance renewal dates etc? At the same time, make sure the immunisation booklet is up to date, and if it isn't, ask the vet to help.

❖ Vets - contact the vets and see if you can be set up on their system for 'text' reminders when appointments are due. One less thing for you to remember.

❖ Perhaps use this time to think carefully about pet insurance if you have not done so?

❖ Have you appointed a 'pet guardian' if you wish to do so?

❖ FILE THE PAPERWORK AWAY

YOUR ACTION POINTS

1:

2:

3:

4:

5:

6:

7:

Chapter 6

People

The pandemic taught us just how much we miss being with people and in particular hugging. Not running up and hugging anyone, but hugging those that mean a lot to us.

When we grew up, we all seemed to see our families more didn't we?

When it comes to people, we don't just mean partners, family, close friends, neighbours and acquaintances.

Let's also think about all those other amazing people in our lives – childminders, gardeners, cleaners, dog walkers, hairdressers, shop owners, car mechanics, the vets, teachers, fitness instructors, the list is endless. And then think about your favourite take-aways, restaurants, clubs. Not identifiable by 'people' but important nonetheless as 'places' so must be included.

All those people that quite simply help us to live our lives. Your wider community!

- Do you have an address book to hand, either physical or online, that stores their information (and is it up to date)?
- Do you have their phone numbers in your phone so you can retrieve their details quickly?
- Have you listed birthdays and anniversaries somewhere so you don't forget?
- Can you get text reminders for appointments? Reach out and see if you can – this means one less thing to think about. Hairdressers, dentists, doctors and so forth.

QUICK WINS

Have an address book so all these details are in one place. It could be online, in a book, or on a spreadsheet, but however you store the information, having it all in one place will mean you can retrieve it with ease and add to it/edit it easily because there will inevitably be changes.

We use the post less and less now but addresses are still useful as well as phone numbers and email addresses.

For any addresses you need to check, why not text/call/WhatsApp the person concerned to find out and at the same time, why not catch up with them?

Remember to update the information as/when it changes. A good time to do this is at Christmas when people often note address changes in their cards. But as changes come in alter as soon as you can.

Create a system whereby you can store birthdays, anniversaries and significant dates so you don't forget them going forwards. For us, every year when we get our new diaries, we transfer all the key dates into the new diary – a fail-proof system for both of us!

Online meetings

There is nothing better than meeting people face to face but there is a place, in this digital age, for meeting online, as the pandemic has shown us. For whatever reason, if you cannot meet up in person, there is now the option for meeting online which at least keeps communication going.

Two popular ones:

Microsoft Teams

https://www.microsoft.com/en-gb/microsoft-teams/download-app

Zoom

https://zoom.us

And also remember on iPhones that you can use the Facetime capability so that you can 'see' who you are talking to.

TIP - Our mobile phones now have the capability to mark our NOK (next of kin) as emergency contacts (ICE – In Case of Emergency). Check this out and how about getting that done too.

TIP - Do you need to note phone numbers for significant others anywhere else in case you lose your phone? Until you can memorise your number, know how to find it on your phone or note it down somewhere in your purse, wallet, notebook. We have both been caught on without knowing both our own numbers and our partner's numbers for example. In this day and age we just click a number, we don't have to remember anything.

TIP – You can now stop all those unwanted calls by opting into the TPS (Telephone Preference Service). It works for us and is well worth doing. Check the website:

https://www.tpsonline.org.uk/tps/whatiscorporatetps.html

TIP – After Christmas gather up cards and well wishes from emails and note who you have received cards from on a spreadsheet or in a notebook. Check the spellings of names and any changes to addresses in the right places. We do love writing family names on cards at Christmas, rather than '... and family' as a cop out when not being able to remember children's names! Keep the list – you can then refer to it next year rather than scratching your head and trying to remember who to send cards to. How organised is that?

REBECCA'S REMINDERS

❖ Make sure you have an address book (online or a physical address book) where you store all your addresses and check that names and addresses up are to date.

❖ It's also worth making a note of any special dates next to their names – birthdays, anniversaries etc. and then diarise the dates so you don't forget.

❖ Are the phone numbers in your phone up to date?

❖ Have you marked who your emergency contacts would be on your phone – ICE?

❖ FILE THE PAPERWORK AWAY

YOUR ACTION POINTS

1:

2:

3:

4:

5:

6:

7:

Chapter 7

Personal Computers

Can you remember when you happened across your first computer?

Tracy – in my 3rd year maths lesson.

Rebecca - we had had our IT lessons at secondary school on BBC Micros.

For many, computers have always been a part of their lives.

We decided to give this subject a chapter of its own. After all, we do so much online, on our phones and tablets now. Indulge us, if you will, a tablet when we were young, was a yukky big white thing you had to swallow when you had a headache or referred to as a bar of soap.

Sensible Precautions

1. **This subject is everchanging with regards safety, security and what we should and should not do online. We have highlighted areas below purely to get you started.**

2. **Do not give your passwords, PINs, memorable information out to anyone.**

3. **Do not click any unknown downloads.**

4. **Do not open any messages from people you don't know.**

5. **The best advice is IF IN DOUBT, DON'T DO ANYTHING. Seek advice.**

Passwords, PINs, two step verification, memorable information, identifying questions to open our accounts... it's endless and ever changing. One chapter alone will not cover or indeed keep up with it all but we want to open up your thinking. It is vital that you follow sound and up to date advice and keep secure.

The 'physical' stuff – iPads, phones, computers, hard drives and laptops. In fact, computer seems such a dated word now doesn't it? This take-over of our lives has MASSIVELY changed the way we live. Who needs Encyclopaedia Britannica? Everything seems to be at our fingertips and we all have a friend in Google.

Also, we now all have, and will leave, our very own 'digital footprint'.

PASSWORDS, PINs AND THOSE SECURITY THINGS

It is important to store these safely so that someone with the wrong intention cannot access them. You don't want to put yourself in a vulnerable position.

Take advantage of all the new security protocols that come in – 2 step verification, fingerprints, for example. This will be ever changing so do keep up to date and follow guidance from the professionals.

- If someone obtains access to your email account, **you are vulnerable**. Think of all the information they will have at their fingertips.
- Software and app updates will often have security updates. It is important that these are done as and when you are notified. If you don't do them, **you are vulnerable.**
- Screen lock your devices. If you don't **you are vulnerable.**
- Back up onto an external hard drive or to a cloud-based facility. If you don't do it, **you are vulnerable**.

We would advise you to take some time to read the information on the following link, from the National Cyber Security Centre (NCSC). The information and guidance does not get any better than this and is easy to read.

https://www.ncsc.gov.uk/collection/top-tips-for-staying-secure-online

This will take you through absolutely everything you need to know with regards your security.

PHYSICAL ASSETS

In this category - computers, iPads, phones, memory sticks, dongles... Please follow the advice from the NCSC in the first instance. We would just add:

- Make sure back-ups are done regularly so that you don't lose files, photos and so forth.
- Anti-virus protection is very important to prevent harmful virus attacks. It needs to be running and working at all times. It will highlight any concerns that may crop up so that you can attend to them.
- Have you considered writing down serial numbers of items in case of loss or theft?
- Have you considered what information is stored on remote hard drives and memory sticks? These must be stored somewhere safe if there is sensitive information on them. It is worth having a think and gathering them all up into one place if you have had many over the years.

A word in particular about mobile phones

Thought needs to be given to the fact that many people now mindlessly upgrade their phones even though they are still fully functioning.

Two things on upgrades:

1. Consider the environment if you upgrade. Do you really need a new phone? Another phone potentially destined for the landfill.
2. Think about the information stored on your old phone when you upgrade. You need to ensure it is all erased. Is it worth replacing 'what ain't broke' at this time?

Now stop for a moment and think about how much of our lives we store on our phones. How we 'can't live' without them? We are carrying around so much personal data.

Notes of caution

We have stressed the importance of information getting into the wrong hands. Consider giving your mobile phones some thought.

- Have your phone password protected.
- Have the screen lock on.
- Use the fingerprint option if you have this.
- Have you got yours insured? So many don't. Phones are not cheap to replace these days.
- Do you know how to contact your provider should the need arise, perhaps if you have lost your phone?
- Do you back your phone up? This is something many people DO NOT think about. Consider what information you are holding on your phone and what you stand to lose.

BACK-UPS

These can be done for computers, laptops, iPads and phones. They can be backed-up onto an external hard drive or cloud-based facility. We would recommend cloud-based back-ups which are stored independently and on the internet. This means that your data will never be lost. The cloud facility will also be backing up your back-ups regularly.

Vital for a couple of key reasons:

1. You don't want to lose your files, contacts, photographs and everything else, if your device is lost or stolen or there was a fire.
2. If your computer has a virus, everything could be damaged and lost. This would not be retrievable without a back-up.

With regular back-ups, even if you are in a situation where you stand to lose everything, you will be able to retrieve your data as long as the back-ups have been kept up to date.

DESTRUCTION

When destroying physical computer items, it is important to seek expert advice on this.

When no longer required, memory sticks and hard drives will need to be destroyed properly. Be mindful of the information that is stored on these items and what damage could be done if this ended up in the wrong hands.

DIGITAL FILING

A suggestion on digital filing but again, find what works for you.

- Create a new folder and name it. Think of it along the lines of physical filing.
- You can create sub-folders within this main folder.
- You are now ready to upload or 'drag' (if you're a Mac user) and file documents.
- Scan documents onto your computer and file them immediately in the relevant folders, as you would for paperwork.
- Remove email attachments and file those in folders if you wish. Or have a filing system within your 'inbox' where you can create your own folders and sub folders and 'drag and drop'.
- Now and again go through and delete old documents and put them in the 'bin'.
- Remember to then 'empty the bin' regularly.

OUR DIGITAL FOOTPRINT LIVES ON

Once we are out there, we are out there in the public domain! Even when we die, our digital footprint will remain. However, with this in mind, you may find the following links extremely useful. As ever, this is in a constant state of flux so do keep referring to the internet for up-to-date advice. At the time of print, we will highlight the following which is correct at the time of going to print.

GOOGLE

Google will close inactive accounts after 2 years of inactivity. It is important, if you have photos or documents stored there, that you 'pop in and out' of your account to keep it 'active'.

So, what is the best way to deal with Google when you die? Just leave your account inactive for them to be deleted and everything lost?

A better way is to use Google's Inactive Account Manager.

https://support.google.com/accounts/answer/3036546?hl=en

This allows you to set specific requests about what is to be done with your account after it has been inactive for a set amount of time. This can be set by you. You retain control, safe in the knowledge that things can be saved and kept by others, if that is your wish.

FACEBOOK

Facebook now have very specific advice on the accounts of the deceased. There is an option to nominate a 'legacy contact', for example. If you want to know more about this, then please follow the link.

https://www.facebook.com/help/103897939701143?rdrhc

TRAINING & SUPPORT

We speak from experience when we say that many people go into a blind panic when it comes to 'back ups', 'virus checkers', 'uploads and downloads'.

We offer training on all things digital in 1:1 situations on Zoom or at client's home and also via downloads and group coaching. There is something for everyone and it can be bespoke to your needs.

Don't feel panic or concern about any of this. Just get in touch via Messenger through the 'Dying to Declutter' Facebook Page and we will help you.

REBECCA'S REMINDERS

❖ Are your usernames, passwords, PIN numbers etc stored somewhere safely?

❖ And are all your devices backed-up – that could be to an external hard drive, or to 'the cloud', or indeed to both.

❖ Do you have virus software installed on your computer? If not, it's easy to get and well worth it.

❖ Are your devices insured?

❖ As with paperwork, any files you store on your computer or your phone are worth filing properly. If your online filing mirrors your offline filing, it can make life much easier – particularly if someone else ever needs to look for something.

❖ Don't forget to delete any digital accounts you no longer use – email accounts, for example.

❖ Destroy your 'hardware' professionally and securely.

❖ Always keep in mind your digital security and safety. If in doubt, seek advice.

❖ Consider making arrangements with Google and Facebook Legacy.

❖ FILE THE PAPERWORK AWAY

YOUR ACTION POINTS

1:

2:

3:

4:

5:

6:

7:

Chapter 8

Pounds & Pennies

And do you know that at one time pennies were shortened to 'd'?
It was named after the Latin word for this coin which was
'denarius'.
And then from 1971 everyone had to learn 'new money'.

Another section in your filing system will be for 'FINANCES'

- Do you know where all your bank accounts are? Think banks, online account providers, building societies, savings accounts, ISAs.

- Many people have dormant accounts (Tracy used to work in a bank and knows this!), so why not seek those out, close them and take the balance, or start using them again?

- For starters there could be some hidden cash that you have forgotten about so if nothing else, this is surely an exercise worth doing.

REMEMBER BANKS AND BUILDING SOCIETIES WILL NEVER ASK YOU FOR PASSWORDS, PINs OR MEMORABLE INFORMATION FOR YOUR ONLINE ACCOUNTS.

The most important thing here is to have a list of bank account providers in one place. You can be pretty limited on the information you note. Allow just enough to point someone in the right direction of the account, when they need to. Again, think about passwords and access and storing that information in a safe place. Remember it is illegal for anyone to access your accounts without legal authorisation.

BANK STATEMENTS

Do you make use of online statements now to save paper and reduce your filing? The planet will love you! You can print statements whenever you wish, or view them online with the need to print.

If you still have paper statements, file them in date order and separated by account – makes it much easier and quicker if you ever have to refer back to one of them. However, do consider switching to online. The information is there at your fingertips whenever you need it without having to wait for the post.

We have touched on PINs and passwords, but it's worth mentioning again here. Have you stored your PINs and passwords securely? And do you change them regularly? Does your trusted person know where to find them for that time of need?

It could be worth considering using an online 'password manager'.

A password manager is a programme that allows users to store, create, and manage their passwords. There are so many to choose from if you wish to store passwords in this way and a Google search will call up current providers.

CREDIT CARDS AND STORE CARDS

Do you have a list of any credit cards held in your name? Check your files and cut up any cards that have expired, or that are attached to an account you no longer hold. Are there any hiding in your wallet, for example?

Whilst checking for credit cards, do you have any store cards? Are there any you are holding that you no longer use? Have you checked to see if you are 'owed' any incentives?

FINANCIAL ADVISOR, BANK MANAGER, MORTGAGE ADVISOR

Do you have anyone in your 'financial tribe'? Are their names and contact details stored somewhere where you can retrieve them easily without going through paperwork? Likewise, with your Accountant, if you have one.

SHARES, PEPS, PREMIUM BONDS

Do you have shares, PEPs, Premium Bonds? Are the share certificates filed safely in your filing system? Do your children have Premium Bonds, Children's Bonds from christening and birthdays for example? Think back and find the documents.

DIRECT DEBITS AND STANDING ORDERS

Do you know what you are paying by direct debit and standing order? And if so, it is worth going through them and deleting what is no longer current as well as checking that you are not paying for anything you shouldn't be and therefore wasting money. If you have an online account, this can be done quickly and easily – a quick win in our book!

Moving forward, we would recommend setting up as much as you can by standing order and direct debit so that you don't have to think about monthly payments on a regular basis (and risk missing a payment).

Standing Order – you can set up direct from your bank account.

Direct Debit – has to be set up via the company you want to pay.

Another quick win is to check your mobile phone apps – are you still be paying for apps that you no longer use?

PAYPAL

Likewise, if you have a PayPal account, are you paying for anything there regularly that you no longer need? It's so easy to forget and not notice those small amounts leaving our accounts, particularly if you don't regularly check your monthly statements.

EXTRAS

Do you owe money to anyone? Is money owed to you? Put a note in the Action pile if so and attend to this when you have time.

Do you have any bank accounts with 'benefits'? For example, travel insurance, mobile phone insurance? Are you paying for benefits you are not even using? Check those out and it may be that you don't need a 'paid for' account.

You should be getting the idea now. Check, check, check and seek, seek, seek, you never know what you may find.

TIP - We love Martin Lewis and his 'money tips' for help and advice with anything 'finance' related, so do find some time to log on for tips and advice. It's well worth it.

https://www.moneysavingexpert.com

TIP – For those who submit tax returns. Why not have a folder or file for this each year. Have a list of what you need to submit so you can gather paperwork up following the list and throughout the year, rather than wasting time trying to remember each year.

REBECCA'S REMINDERS

❖ File finance related paperwork and create a digital file for any scanned documents (if relevant).

❖ View bank statements online and only print if necessary – the planet will thank you!

❖ It's useful to have your accountant / financial advisor's details stored in the file too.

❖ Don't forget to keep your passwords and PIN numbers safe and change them regularly. Or use a password manager.

❖ Search out and keep a list of all your bank accounts, PEPs, Premium Bonds etc in your filing system (including those belonging to your children) so you know exactly where all your accounts are.

❖ As an extra bonus, this list will be useful if you move house and need to notify people of your new address.

❖ FILE THE PAPERWORK AWAY

YOUR ACTION POINTS

1:

2:

3:

4:

5:

6:

7:

Chapter 9

Possessions

Do we really need all the 'stuff' we have these days?
Having less 'stuff', helps give us more headspace.

So here we are in another section in your filing system entitled 'POSSESSIONS'. We will split this into household items and vehicles. If you have caravans, motor homes, boats, jewellery etc. you may wish to do separate sections for those, depending on how much paperwork you have. The key thing is to make it easy to find everything when you need it.

It may be worth considering doing an inventory at some point, if you wish. This can be written in a notebook or on a spreadsheet again, making sure your trusted person knows there this is held. Noting values of items and also supporting this with photographs means that, in the event of a loss or damage, you will have everything that an insurance company will need for a claim, they will thank you for having this to hand. A gold star moment! Add in serial numbers and purchase receipts, your life will be so much more straightforward should you need to make a claim.

HOUSEHOLD ITEMS

- Do you have your possessions/contents insured? Remember that buildings insurance is different to contents insurance.

- Do you have photographs of items of value safely stored, for insurance purposes? This is for 'every day' items such as bicycles as well as jewellery, artwork and other valuables. Have you noted any important item identification numbers?

- Do you have insurance valuation certificates (market value) and provenance details for valuable items such as jewellery, artwork, and furniture? Are they in date? Do these certificates expire?

- Receipts and Guarantees - only hang on to these if they are still valid. Receipts are usually valid for 30 days but beyond that they are only proof of purchase. Many shops now hold guarantees/receipts online for customers, John Lewis as one such store. Check your paperwork and file any still in date.

TIP – Valuable items. Check your insurance policy covers all of these items.

TIP – Valuation Certificates. These 'may' expire (see your insurance Ts & Cs). It's important to make sure they're up to date because if you make a claim, some insurers will not pay out if the Certificate is out of date.

It would be remiss of us not to mention 'decluttering' when it comes to possessions. This is covered by so many wonderful people including the lovely Marie Kondo and Stacey Solomon. We don't need to add anything to this other than, decluttering is good for the soul and worth finding time for but only when your paperwork is in order!

Finally, with contents insurance, do check every year that you are adequately covered. What has changed in the last year? Have you acquired anything else? Has any item increased in value? Maybe you purchased some jewellery on holiday - remember when you get home to add this to your insurance policy.

Now back to the paperwork.

VEHICLES

- Do you have insurance that is adequate for use and in date? Check what is not covered. Does your vehicle need to be garaged over-night, for example? Are you covered for business use?
- Do you know where the V5 is, known as the logbook?
- Do you have breakdown insurance? Does it cover all of your vehicles/drivers?

- Do you have spare keys put away somewhere safe?
- Is your car tax due for renewal? Further details can be obtained by following the link:

  https://www.gov.uk/vehicle-tax

- Is your MOT in date? Further details can be obtained by following the link:

  https://www.gov.uk/getting-an-mot

- Do you know your registration number? Have you ever arrived at the parking meter only to have to walk back to check the registration number? We have a photo on our phones that we refer to. Top tip!
- Driving licence? Do you know where it is? Does it need an address change? Please follow the link below for help and advice if so. It is important that this is kept up to date.

  https://www.gov.uk/browse/driving/driving-licences

- Are all of these documents now filed safely either digitally or in your paper filing system?
- Diarise any key dates – insurance renewal, MOT, tax, servicing.
- Check with your garage to see if they will send you MOT and servicing reminders so they are not forgotten.

- Do you have any Blue Badge parking or are you eligible? More details can be found by following this link.

  https://www.gov.uk/apply-blue-badge

REBECCA'S REMINDERS

❖ This is a big section so why not 'chunk it down' so you can deal with it in stages?

❖ Keep an inventory (along with photos) of any items of value. Aside from the fact that should you ever need to make an insurance claim you have all the information to hand, it is also very useful to know exactly what you have, it's value and so forth.

❖ As a thought, is there anything on this list that you may want to gift when you pass away? If so, make sure it's written into your Will or written separately and filed with your Will. Seek professional advice on this.

❖ Is all relevant paperwork filed and up to date? That includes your contents insurance, valuation certificates, car insurance, car documentation etc.

❖ Have you noted any key dates in your diary? Most garages have a reminder system that can notify you when your car is due for a service or MOT, so do make sure you sign up for that.

❖ Don't forget to save a photo of your car registration number on your phone – just in case!

❖ Is all your vehicle paperwork up-to-date and the car roadworthy and legal?

❖ FILE THE PAPERWORK AWAY

YOUR ACTION POINTS

1:

2:

3:

4:

5:

6:

7:

Chapter 10

'Ployment (aka work)

Who remembers paper rounds on their bikes?

Dreading the weekend with the heavy Sunday supplements and not

being able to get them in the letterbox? The shoulder problems in

later life from those heavy paper bags.

Another section in your filing system will be for 'WORK' or 'EMPLOYMENT'

The Government website has a lot of information on being employed, status and regulations.

https://www.gov.uk/employment-status/employee

If you are employed by a company and have any problems, your HR Office/representative should be able to help. For those who are self-employed, you can refer online to ACAS, depending on the issue at hand. ACAS provides free impartial advice.

https://www.acas.org.uk

So, let's gather up what we need.

EMPLOYED

- If employed, do you know where your employment contract is?
- Do you keep your payslips or know how to access them online?
- Whether employed or self-employed, make sure you keep any Government documentation like your P45, P11D, P60 and self-assessment forms, for example. An explanation of these can be found by following the link:

  https://www.gov.uk/paye-forms-p45-p60-p11d

- If you have a company pension, do you know the details for this?

SELF EMPLOYED

- If self-employed do you retain invoices that you issue to clients, expense receipts, supplier invoices and put them in a safe place, ready for your tax return? This is crucial.
- Do you have your Accountant's details stored and accessible and have a good working relationship with them? Do you

have regular meetings with them to ensure you are doing the best you can with your financial affairs?

- If you're self-employed, are your insurance documents up to date?
- Are you keeping a track of invoices, expenses and so forth for your tax return?

TIP – For those of you having to do tax returns, are you collating the necessary paperwork month by month? We have a great checklist and each month we gather together what we will need at the Year End. At the time of your tax return, the majority of your paperwork will already be in one place and ready to process.

CV

- Do you know where your education and qualification certificates are?
- Do you have a CV that is up to date – if applicable?
- Have you got references stored?

REBECCA'S REMINDERS

❖ If you're employed, make sure all the relevant paperwork is stored together – employment contract, payslips, HMRC documentation, NI number. You never know when you might need to refer to it, so have it in one place.

❖ If you're self-employed, do you have any relevant qualification certificates filed, your insurance paperwork (is it up to date?), any receipts and documentation for your tax return?

❖ If you still need a CV, keep it updated and with your educational certificates and any references.

❖ FILE THE PAPERWORK AWAY

YOUR ACTION POINTS

1:

2:

3:

4:

5:

6:

7:

Chapter 11

Pensions / Insurances

It's never too early to think about pensions and insurances.

If there is one piece of advice we would pass to the younger

generation, it would be to get sound financial advice earlier on in

life.

Another section in your filing system will be for 'PENSIONS & INSURANCES'

Seek professional advice on personal pensions and insurances.

We are just here to get the filing done

As we start out in life, retirement seems so far away and before you know it, here it is just around our corner. Where did the time go? And now we truly understand the saying that 'youth is wasted on the young'!

- Many of us will have pensions. For example, state, work, widows, military, private pensions. If you have any of these, do you know where the information about each one is? Do you know their worth? Do you have the company details noted along with account numbers?
- State Pensions – you can check what yours is worth and then have a good idea about future requirements and if you need to do any 'topping up'. Please click the link below:

https://www.gov.uk/check-state-pension

- Do you have a pension advisor? If so, do you have their contact details? If you don't, ask around for recommendations.
- It's always worth regularly checking your pension provisions.
- Endowment policies, critical illness policies. If you have these do you have the details and company names? Are they in date? Do they still cover what is necessary? Check that they do, this is very important. Always make sure you review policies every year when they come up for renewal.
- Do you have life insurance or life assurance policy? Is it / are they in date? Do they cover what you need them to cover?

Critical Illness insurance - this policy covers you if you become critically ill during the term of the policy.

Life Assurance – this will pay out a tax-free lump sum if you die whilst the policy is in force.

Life Insurance – this is 'whole life' cover.

Both life assurance and life insurance provide some cover in the event of death.

REBECCA'S REMINDERS

❖ Consider whether you should seek some financial advice. It is often free so shop around.

❖ Is all your paperwork relating to pensions filed together? If you have several pensions, file them separately and in date order. We find it helpful too to have a summary sheet in the file that lists out the name of each pension, where it is held and what it's worth.

❖ Have you looked at what your State Pension is worth? If not, have a look at the gov.uk website – it's very straightforward and a great tool for planning ahead.

❖ Is all your life insurance / life assurance paperwork filed and up to date? It's worth double checking that the cover is correct too – have your circumstances changed since you took the policy out, for example?

❖ When needing professional advice, it is always good to ask for recommendations.

❖ FILE THE PAPERWORK AWAY

YOUR ACTION POINTS

1:

2:

3:

4:

5:

6:

7:

Chapter 12

Property

There really is no place like home.

Another section in your filing system will be for 'PROPERTY'.

This applies to your home whether you own or rent property. It will all require paperwork of some sort.

PROPERTY OWNERS

- Do you know who your mortgage provider is? Do you have the contact and account details (mortgage number) to hand in your file? When is your mortgage due for renewal? In advance of the renewal date do you have a diary note to seek a better mortgage rate deal?

- Are you holding other legal documentation for your house in one place? Deeds can be stored out of the way somewhere safe, if need be, as it's unlikely you'll need to access them regularly (don't forget to write down where you've put them). As well as all the purchasing and solicitors paperwork, for example.

- Do you know where the solicitor's details are should you need to ask questions about deeds or need legal advice at any time? An example might be a fencing dispute where you may need legal advice.

- Is your house insurance up to date? Both buildings and contents? Have you stored the paperwork so you can find it quickly if required? When is the renewal date? Remember, both are different forms of insurance.

- Utilities - have you noted your providers along with the account numbers? This could be a note on an A4 piece of paper, handwritten and filed in the property section of your filing system or on a spreadsheet? Any way will suffice as long as it works for you.

- Make a note somewhere of who holds your spare keys. Are they with a trusted neighbour? Can you even account for all your key sets? Do you need a key safe at the property?

- Alarm - does a trusted person have the code? Do you have the code stored safely somewhere? Do you have the security company details listed in your contacts in case you need it?

RENTAL PROPERTIES

TENANT

- If you rent, do you have your tenancy documentation filed?
- Do you have a call out number for emergencies from your landlord or letting agent?
- Are you getting receipts or invoices for rent due?

LANDLORD

- Do you retain all the paperwork for income and expenses for your tax return?
- Are you ensuring your rental property is compliant? This is ever changing and advice can be obtained from the following link:

https://www.gov.uk/renting-out-a-property

UTILITIES

TIP – Get the renewal dates for your utilities and put a diary note in for 3 months before so that you can start looking for a better deal. You will then be ahead of the game; this is the time when you can get a better deal. If you leave it to the last minute you might miss out on a good deal.

If you shop earlier rather than later Martin Lewis will be so proud of you, so please refer to his website for help and guidance.

https://www.moneysavingexpert.com

Below is a list of this basic information, for bills and queries. There is a download for this sheet on our Facebook Page.

You may want to create copies if you have other properties too.

Property Address:

....

Electricity Provider

Account Number   ....

Telephone Number   ....

Gas Provider

Account Number   ....

Telephone Number   ....

Water Provider

Account Number   ....

Telephone Number   ....

Council Tax – Local Authority

Account Number   ....

Telephone Number   ....

TV Licence Number   ....

Telephone Provider

Account Number   ....

Telephone Number   ....

Broadband Provider

Account Number   ....

Telephone Number   ....

Mobile Provider

Account Number   ....

Telephone Number   ....

TV/Sat TV/ Cable Provider

Account Number   ....

Telephone Number   ....

IN CASE OF EMERGENCY NUMBERS

Below is a useful list that you might like to complete so that you have these numbers to hand. Also put them in your phone if that will help you. There is a download for this document on our Facebook Page (see the link at the end of the book). Please add more numbers that are relevant.

- Electricity: ....

- Gas: ....

- Water: ....

- Electrician: ....

- Plumber: ....

- Carpenter: ....

Other Useful (property related) Numbers:

....

....

....

Where is the stopcock located? ....

Where is the electricity/gas meter? ....

Do you know how to turn off the electricity and gas? YES/NO (if no, then please find out).

REBECCA'S REMINDERS

❖ Is all legal documentation including mortgages and/or rental agreements filed away?

❖ Are your solicitor's details recorded in case of need, for example, a fencing and boundary dispute?

❖ House and contents insurance up to date and filed? Ensure it is checked annually and that there are no exclusions added on by the insurance company that you now need to be aware of.

❖ Utilities – bills filed for one year only if required and renewal dates logged with a date a few months beforehand to start 'shopping around' for the best deals.

❖ Spare keys held with someone else in case of need?

❖ Alarm - does a trusted person have the code?

❖ If you have rental properties ensure these are complaint. Legislation is ever changing.

❖ Consider filing the information and emergency sheets somewhere accessible in the house for ease of reference.

❖   FILE THE PAPERWORK AWAY

YOUR ACTION POINTS

1:

2:

3:

4:

5:

6:

7:

Chapter 13

Pleasure & Leisure

Time outside is good for the soul.

It boosts your energy, your immune system and gives you a daily

dose of Vitamin D.

As we grew up we were outside all day long, in the mud, rain,

whatever!

So, we are nearly there and what a great topic this is after some of the others, don't you think?

A 'PLEASURE/LEISURE' section is now required if this is relevant to you. The classic case is the gym membership bought with good intention in the New Year. And by February, is no longer being used but still being paid for in August!

Be aware of what you are committing to and paying for.

- Do you know where your passport is, if you have one, and is it in date? If you have lost it, or need to renew it, here is the link:

  https://www.gov.uk/apply-renew-passport

- Travel insurance? Is it in date and do you have the insurance document to hand? Always check the insurance is valid before you travel, and the right insurance for your trips. Thinking here of skiing trips, hazardous pursuits. If you have any change in medical conditions, that must be advised too.

- Vaccination records for travel. Are these up to date? Please check the link below in good time before you travel: https://www.nhs.uk/conditions/travel-vaccinations/

- Airline membership schemes such as the old fashioned 'Airmiles' are worth investigating and using up if you have accumulated any points of value. They often go out of date so if they can be used, why not.

TIP – if planning any trips overseas, check whether visas and vaccinations are required, well before you travel. This can take time to put in place.

- Are you a member of any sports clubs or gyms? Are you still going to these facilities? Are you paying for other clubs or memberships that you are no longer using? Cancel and stop paying. Save yourself some money.

- Points, store and discount cards. If you have any cards that collect points or offer discounts, do you know where they are? Do you even use them to save yourself money? Are they in date?

- Concerts, theatre, events. Do you have tickets for any and if so, do you know where they are? Do you know the cancellation terms?

- Are you paying for any children's activities that they are no longer doing?

- Scour bank statements and check you are not paying anything unnecessarily with regards leisure activities.

- Volunteer work. Are you still doing this? Have you stopped for some reason? If not, why not let them know you are no longer available and remove your details from their system. Or, why not get out again and start. It's a great way to be with people and to do something beneficial.

- Retirement associations, unions, military organisations?

- Magazine/newspaper subscriptions. Are you still paying for magazines or newspapers you are not reading (or enjoying)? If so, make sure you cancel these to save money (and clutter!). Or perhaps subscribe to online reading material.

- The list is endless but exhaust everything. Cancel what you are no longer using to save money.

DIGITAL LEISURE

At the risk of stating the obvious, there is so much you can do online now. From books to read as well as audible versions. Magazines and newspapers. Social media. Online courses. The list is extensive. Have you finished those courses you signed up for? Are you paying for anything unnecessarily?

REBECCA'S REMINDERS

❖ Is your passport in date?

❖ Is your travel insurance up to date and does it cover you for what you need? Do you know where your vaccination documents are if you need to travel? Have you checked in good time, that you have the right vaccinations?

❖ Are there any memberships (including for airlines), store cards etc that you're still paying for that you're no longer using? If so, work through them and cancel them (don't forget to unsubscribe to online newsletters too while you're at it).

❖ Magazines/newspapers are easy to overlook too – are you reading them? Do you enjoy them, or are they just piling up on the side, unread? If so, cancel them.

❖ As things arrive through the letterbox or into your inbox, consider their usefulness and if you still need them. If not, cancel them.

❖ Have you got a safe place to keep theatre, opera or festival tickets, or do you know where they are saved digitally? There is nothing worse than a last-minute scramble searching for them!

❖ FILE THE PAPERWORK AWAY

YOUR ACTION POINTS

1:

2:

3:

4:

5:

6:

7:

Chapter 14

Probate

The very essence of the work we are doing is to try to ease this process by having everything in one place and easily retrievable.

When a person dies and leaves behind their property and possessions, which is referred to as their 'Estate', someone needs to deal with this. The process is called Probate.

Further information and advice can be found:

https://www.moneysavingexpert.com/family/guide-to-probate/

This is another section where we recommend that you seek professional advice.

But we will get you started by providing an overview on Wills and Lasting Power of Attorneys (LPAs).

WILL

A Will is a legal document that spells out your final wishes regarding the inheritance of your property, your finances, the care of your children after your death. It is made voluntarily aged 18 or over. You also instruct executor(s) who you have nominated to carry out your wishes.

It is important that we leave a Will for many reasons and one being, again, to alleviate the inevitable distress that arises when this has not been done. Not only will it cause emotional upset but it will delay and protract the process and particularly for those you care about most.

While you can write your Will yourself using online templates, or 'Will kits' from stationery shops, if it's not straightforward it's worth seeking professional advice through a solicitor or a professional will writer. Once it is written, it'll need to be formally witnessed and signed – this makes it a legally binding document. It then needs to be stored safely. Your Solicitor or Will Writer can do this for you, or if you do it yourself, you'll need to store it safely. Make sure you have a copy of it for your own records.

Don't forget that you can update or change your Will – you can either make an official alteration (called a 'codicil') or start from scratch and make a new Will. There are options to go to a solicitor, do it online or hire a qualified Will writer.

Further information and advice can be obtained from this website.

https://www.gov.uk/make-will

LASTING POWER OF ATTORNEY (LPA)

In very simple terms, this is a legal document that allows you to appoint someone to make decisions on your behalf. There are two types – health and welfare, and property and financial affairs.

Health and Welfare LPA – if someone cannot deal with decisions about their health and care then this will come into effect.

Property and Financial Affairs LPA – allows for someone to deal with your financial matters such as paying bills, accessing bank accounts, changing utilities, moving house. This can be used, if need be, as soon as it is registered, but only with your written permission.

It is worth bearing in mind that there are many things that may be in a husband/partner's name and when it comes to needing to make changes, without an LPA, these will be difficult or impossible to implement.

It's easy and straightforward to arrange both of these yourself through the gov.uk website (https://www.gov.uk/power-of-attorney). Or you can ask your solicitor to arrange everything for you.

SPECIAL CHERISHED POSSESSIONS

We thought we would add a quick paragraph on this. We have both experienced different ways of doing this. Some people write a list that they put in with their Will. Some have the items specified formally in their Will for certain people. Life changes, so a signed note alongside your Will is often the best way so this can be updated with ease. However, do take advice on this first particularly when it comes to highly valuable items.

As we have alluded to a member of Rebecca's family has put stickers on items such as pictures, paintings, ornaments, with the name of the person that it is to be left too.

Tracy has been given a cherished sentimental item by her mother. A gold bangle that was no longer worn but very special to her mum. It was kept in a box but has now given a new lease of life being enjoyed by Tracy and also by her mum seeing, the joy it has given Tracy.

REBECCA'S REMINDERS

❖ This is a short introduction into something that we feel is very important. Something many people put off, just won't do, or think *'it won't happen to me'*. Stop and think about what would happen **IF** something were to happen to you and you had none of these things in place.

❖ **IN THE FIRST INSTANCE, SEEK PROFESSIONAL ADVICE.**

❖ If you haven't written your Will yet, no matter how young or old you are, please get the ball rolling – it's straightforward to do. If you have, then that's great. Just make sure it's a) up to date, and b) you have a copy in your files and know where the original is stored (with a note left in your files so your next of kin can find it).

❖ Have you appointed your LPAs (for both Health & Welfare, and Property & Finance)? Don't forget to make a note of your LPA contact details in your files.

❖ Have you thought about marking items you wish to bequeath or gifting whilst still alive, those items that are no longer used, put away until such time?

❖ Tell your trusted person where your Will is store.

❖   FILE THE PAPERWORK AWAY

YOUR ACTION POINTS

1:

2:

3:

4:

5:

6:

7:

Chapter 15

Popping Your Clogs

Rebecca had an aunt who put stickers on her valuable items. On the stickers she had written the names of those she wished those items to be bequeathed to. Rebecca used to sneak peeks when she went around for tea hoping that the ghastly china ladies were not coming her way!

So why have we written this book?

To get you organised and to give you back precious time so you can live the life you want and to its fullest.

Also, because… when you pass away, those you leave behind will know where to find everything they need to deal with on your departure. It will all be in one place and we now urge you to tell someone you trust, of this place so that they are aware of it.

All that needs to be said is 'if anything happens, everything you need is located …'.

With this in mind, earlier in the book, we mentioned the 'Tell us Once' service for which you will need personal information with which to be able to access it.

TELL US ONCE

'Tell Us Once' is a service that lets you report a death to most UK government organisations in one go. Do use it – it will save you so much time and stress.

https://www.gov.uk/after-a-death/organisations-you-need-to-contact-and-tell-us-once

Before you use Tell Us Once, you'll need the following details of the person who died:

- Date of birth
- National Insurance number
- Driving licence number (if applicable)
- Vehicle registration number (if applicable)
- Passport number
- The date they passed away

If you have followed our process you will have the all the records and paperwork in place.

You'll also need:

- Details of any benefits or entitlements they were getting - for example State Pension.
- Details of any local council services they were getting - for example Blue Badge.
- Name, address, telephone number and the National Insurance number or date of birth of any surviving spouse or civil partner.
- Name and address of their next of kin - if there is no surviving spouse or civil partner or their spouse or civil partner is not able to deal with their affairs.
- Name, address and contact details of the person or company dealing with their estate (property, belongings and money), known as their 'executor' or 'administrator'.
- Details of any public sector or armed forces pension schemes they were getting or paying in to.
- You need permission from any surviving spouse or civil partner, the next of kin, executor, administrator or anyone who was claiming joint benefits or entitlements with the person who died, before you give their details.

This service is so useful and coupled with an organised paperwork system, will make life so much less stressful for those dealing with the affairs of the departed.

REBECCA'S REMINDERS

❖ Is your Will up to date and stored safely? Would your next of kin know where to find it? Have you included a list of things you would like to gift to friends and family?

❖ Do you have LPAs in place for **both** your Property and Finance, as well as your Health and Welfare? Is the paperwork up to date and filed safely?

❖ Does your trusted person now know where everything is stored?

❖ Is everything in place for 'Tell Us Once'?

❖ FILE THE PAPERWORK AWAY

YOUR ACTION POINTS

1:

2:

3:

4:

5:

6:

7:

And breathe ...

Now you will have:

All of your paperwork stored safely in one place.

Someone you trust who knows where this paperwork is stored.

Someone you trust who knows where your passwords, PINs, access codes are stored, if stored separately.

Someone you trust who knows where your long-term documentation, like deeds, are stored, if stored separately.

A system is in place to ensure all documentation is kept up to date.

A diary note is in place to check in on your paperwork from time to time to ensure it is always up to date.

Your Will and LPA(s) are in place.

Postscript

Do you remember writing at school and always having to end with a 'conclusion'?

Well, this is our conclusion.

This book, or project, very much evolved as it went along.

As you know now, what started out as a book about 'organising your paperwork' took us on a very different journey.

With that in mind, if there is just one thing you take from our book, let it be that you consider what would happen if you or your other half suddenly died. Would either of you, or indeed your family, know where to begin with regards finding the necessary paperwork?

As we said at the start of this book, 'Popping your clogs' is inevitable but being organised is a choice, and this choice will affect your nearest and dearest at one of the worst times in their lives.

Live a fabulously organised and fun life!

Thank you for reading our book, and let us know how you get on. We would love to keep in touch with you.

With love, Rebecca and Tracy

Additional Information

If you would like to keep in touch with us, please use the link below and in return for your email address we'll send you the checklists from within the book.

https://mailchi.mp/065b62d285c5/dying-to-declutter

Related Links

https://www.facebook.com/Dying-to-Declutter-102879338531059

https://www.moonpig.com

https://www.Paperlesspost.com

https://www.jacquielawson.com

https://www.trello.com

https://www.todoist.com

https://www.mcafee.com

https://www.norton.com

https://www.bitdefender.com

https://www.gov.uk/order-copy-birth-death-marriage-certificate

https://www.gov.uk/national-insurance/your-national-insurance-number

https://www.nhs.uk/using-the-nhs/about-the-nhs/what-is-an-nhs-number/

https://www.nhs.uk/nhs-services/prescriptions-and-pharmacies/the-nhs-website-repeat-prescription-ordering-service/

https://www.tpp-uk.com/products/airmid

https://www.coop.co.uk/health

https://www.evergreen-life.co.uk/

https://www.mygp.com/

https://patally.co.uk/

https://www.patientaccess.com/

https://www.tpp-uk.com/products/systmonline

https://www.boots.com/online/pharmacy/

https://www.echo.co.uk/

https://www.pharmacy2u.co.uk/

https://www.organdonation.nhs.uk/get-involved/news/organ-donation-law-change-due-to-come-into-effect-in-england-on-20th-may

https://www.nhs.uk

https://www.gov.uk/caring-for-pets

https://www.gov.uk/get-your-dog-microchipped

https://www.microsoft.com/en-gb/microsoft-teams/download-app

https://zoom.us

https://www.tpsonline.org.uk/tps/whatiscorporatetps.html

https://www.ncsc.gov.uk/collection/top-tips-for-staying-secure-online

https://support.google.com/accounts/answer/3036546?hl=en

https://www.facebook.com/help/103897939701143?rdrhc

https://www.moneysavingexpert.com

https://www.gov.uk/vehicle-tax

https://www.gov.uk/getting-an-mot

https://www.gov.uk/browse/driving/driving-licences

https://www.gov.uk/apply-blue-badge

https://www.gov.uk/employment-status/employee

https://www.acas.org.uk

https://www.gov.uk/paye-forms-p45-p60-p11d

https://www.gov.uk/check-state-pension

https://www.gov.uk/renting-out-a-property

https://www.moneysavingexpert.com

https://www.gov.uk/apply-renew-passport

https://www.moneysavingexpert.com/family/guide-to-probate/

https://www.gov.uk/make-will

https://www.gov.uk/power-of-attorney

https://www.gov.uk/after-a-death/organisations-you-need-to-contact-and-tell-us-once

Printed in Great Britain
by Amazon